LIFE SKILLS™

HANDBOOKS

21st CENTURY

Community
Resources

Joanne Suter

and

Susan M. Freese

SADDLEBACK
EDUCATIONAL PUBLISHING

ISBN-13: 978-1-61651-689-5
ISBN-10: 1-61651-689-5
eBook: 978-1-61247-341-3

Printed in Guangzhou, China
1111/CA21101811

16 15 14 13 12   1 2 3 4 5

Contents

Your Taxes at Work

You may think about paying taxes every time you look at your paycheck. But do you ever think about all the things that taxes pay for? Taxes pay for the wide range of services offered by the government. That includes schools, parks, and libraries, along with the police and fire departments and even the military. Learn about the services available to you and how they make your life better and safer.

Spending Less While Doing More

Malea was happy to be going back to college. She'd dropped out two years ago. At that time, she'd felt as though she didn't really know what she wanted to do.

Now, Malea knew she wanted to be a pharmacy assistant. It would take two years to get her degree. But after that, she was sure to get a good job, her instructors told her.

While going to school, Malea would have to cut back her hours at work. And working fewer hours would mean earning less money. She'd saved enough to pay for college. Even so, she'd have to cut back her spending a lot.

One of the ways Malea planned to cut back was in buying books. She loved to read! Buying new books was expensive, though. Also, no one but her read most of the books she bought. That made buying them seem wasteful, in a way.

Malea decided to visit the public library. She learned she could check out books for free. She'd have to sign up on a waiting list to get the newest and most popular books. But the wait time wasn't usually more than a week or so.

6

During one of her trips to the library, Malea saw a poster about activities at a local park. There were concerts throughout the summer—all of them free. There were also other free events, including an art fair, a food festival, and a farmers' market.

Malea had never known there were so many things to do in her community—so many free things, especially.

CHAPTER **1**

Public Resources

City, county, state, and ***federal*** governments provide a range of services for their citizens. Do you know about what services are available in your community?

One of the best ways to locate public ***resources*** is to look in the local phone book or online directory. Usually, special pages provide phone numbers for government ***agencies***. In the phone book, these pages are usually blue.

Federal	Resource	Agency
The national level of government.	Something that can be used for information or support.	A business or organization that provides a service to another business or organization.

A Range of Public Services

The following sections show some of the public services you'll probably see listed. Be sure to check for the same services under city, county, state, and federal governments.

Armed Services

Air Force/Department of Air National Guard	Marine Corps
	National Guard
Army/Department of Coast Guard	Navy

The National Guard: Always Ready, Always There

The National Guard is a state-level, reserve military force. That means its members are available when called on to protect people and property. The National Guard provides help during emergencies, such as storms and floods. It responds when called to duty by the US president or the state governor. National Guard units provide help locally in their own states, across the nation, and even around the world.

National Guard members are sometimes called "citizen soldiers." They serve in the Guard part-time and also have full-time jobs. To join, you must be a US citizen and a legal, permanent resident. You must also be age 17 to 35 and meet physical and moral requirements. Training involves one weekend each month and one two-week session each year. Guard members are paid and have the opportunity to learn new skills.

Certificates, Licenses, and Permits

Birth and death certificates

Driver's licenses

Fish and wildlife licenses

Marriage licenses

Motor vehicle plates and registrations

Passports

Community Services

Abuse and assault hotlines

Airports

Animal control

Better Business Bureau (BBB)

Chamber of Commerce

Employment assistance

Fire department

Food stamps program

Garbage collection

Handicapped services

Highways

Housing

Neighborhood associations

Parks and recreation

Public libraries

Public transportation

Recycling

Senior citizen services

Unemployment

Veterans' services

Government

City hall

Courts

Drug enforcement

Governor's office

Post office

Social Security office

Voter registration/information

Chambers of Commerce

- Looking for business opportunities or connections in your area?
- Want to help at a community event?
- Concerned about challenges facing businesses in your neighborhood?
- Interested in improving local schools and other institutions?
- Moving to a new city or town?
- Planning a trip to a place you've never visited before?

Chambers of Commerce connect people in these and many other situations. Chambers exist at the local, regional, state, national, and even international levels. Any time you have a question about a place, it's a good idea to start with the area Chamber of Commerce. And if it can't help you, it probably will know who can.

Education

City, county, and state colleges and universities

Community education programs

Public kindergartens and elementary schools

Public middle schools and high schools

Health and Human Services

Aging and disability

Communicable disease control

Emergency medical services

Environmental health

Food handlers' programs

Health care provider licensing
boards

Medicare

Neighborhood health clinics

Travelers' clinics

Hotlines for these services:
mental health, poison control,
alcohol information, communicable diseases, teen health, and
suicide prevention

Law Enforcement

City police department

County sheriff's office

State patrol

Federal Bureau of Investigation
(FBI)

Crime prevention agency

Weather

Weather service

Road and weather conditions

Outdoor Sirens

Outdoor sirens warn people to find shelter immediately. The three signals that can be used mean these things:

1. A **single tone** that lasts three to five minutes is used for severe weather, such as a tornado. The siren may mean that a storm is occurring or that one is likely to occur. This signal is also used in case a chemical or other dangerous material is spilled.

2. A **two-toned siren** warns of an attack, as in a war.

3. A **faster two-toned siren** alternates between high and low pitches. Communities that have volunteer firefighters use this signal to call firefighters to fires.

CHAPTER **2**

Library Services

Lisa is a teen **volunteer** at her community's public library. She's **impressed** by all the services the library offers.

"It's about more than just books!" Lisa explains. "The library is about sharing information, ideas, and entertainment!"

Lisa is part of a **campaign** for library funding. She's urging citizens to vote for the new funding plan. In the speech on pages 16 and 17, she points out that the library is one of the community's most valuable resources.

Volunteer	Impress	Campaign
Someone who provides a service to an organization for free.	To have a strong, positive effect on.	A plan for trying to get people to vote in favor of something, such as a law, a person, or a program.

Making the Most of Your Local Library

How can you learn about the materials and services available at your local library?

- Go the library's Web site, which explains its services, resources, and guidelines.

- If you don't already have a library card, get one. Ask to fill out an application. Bring along a photo ID and proof of your current address.

- Check the community calendar for events, meetings, training sessions, and other free activities.

- Take advantage of training sessions on computer programs.

- Use what's called *interlibrary loan services* to borrow materials from other libraries.

- Look over the collection of movies, TV shows, and musical recordings.

- Ask one of the librarians! They're there to help you.

Good afternoon, ladies and gentlemen, boys and girls:

How many of you have a library card? Good for you! And for those of you who don't, I have to say that you're missing a great value!

Library cards are free to the people who live in the area. To get one, just come into the library and fill out a form. Then show your driver's license or student ID—something that shows your address. Once you get your card, you can enjoy using the library's wide range of materials and services.

Books, DVDs and CDs, podcasts, magazines, computer software, audiotapes, pamphlets, and even artwork and tools—you can borrow them all from your library. And there's even more!

Do you have a question or need help with research? Get answers from the reference staff in person, by phone, or by computer. Also check out the library's Web sites. It offers endless amounts of information. And an online catalog lists and describes thousands of books and other materials.

Another link lets you research anything from the arts to community activities to the weather. Online book lists help you select things to read. Special Web pages are designed for seniors, for children, and for people who speak languages other than English.

What else does your library offer? Check out the monthly calendar of events! You'll find author visits, book discussions, homework helpers, story times, and art exhibits. You'll also find meeting rooms for free use by community groups. If you don't have a home computer, you can use the library's public computers and Internet access. Job seekers can check the want ads online and in newspapers from cities all around the country.

And remember that all these services are free! Your library card is your key to the kingdom of information.

So when you vote next month, vote "yes" for the library funding plan!

What's in the Reference Section?

The reference section of the library is a "mine" full of information. Reference materials can't usually be checked out. But someone called a *reference librarian* will be available to help: in person, over the phone, and even online. He or she helps guide people to the information they need and shows them how to use these kinds of resources:

- **Print resources:** Dictionaries, encyclopedias, almanacs, atlases, guidebooks, manuals, newspapers, magazines, directories, and other printed materials

- **Electronic resources:** Computers with Internet connection, searchable online databases, free access to thousands of online reference materials

- **Government documents:** Tax forms, the *Congressional Record*, census records, immigration documents, and other references published by local, state, and federal government

The Online Catalog

All of the materials found in the library are recorded in an online database. That database, which is called the *online catalog*, is like a map. It tells you what items the library has, where to find each one, and how to get it. If an item isn't available, you can sign up on a waiting list. Someone from the library will contact you when the item is available.

To find materials in the library, you can search the online catalog in four main ways: by author, by title, by subject, or by using a keyword. You can even search the online catalog from your computer at home.

CHAPTER **3**

Post Office Services

Carlos, like millions of other people, sends letters, **documents**, and packages through the US Postal Service. Some of his letters and packages go to friends and relatives. Other items are sent for business purposes.

Mailing Methods

At the post office, Carlos has a number of choices about mailing methods. The method he chooses for each letter or package depends on several things:

→ The purpose of the mailing

→ The contents of the letter or package

→ Where the item is being mailed

→ How fast it needs to get there

→ The cost of the postage

Usually, the bigger and heavier the item, the more it costs to mail. Also, the faster the item needs to get to its destination, the more it costs to send it.

The charts on pages 24–25 show some of the mailing choices offered by the US Postal Service. These are all ***domestic*** services, which means

Documents
Printed materials that provide information or serve as records. Legal papers and financial records are examples of documents.

Domestic
Belonging to or relating to a specific country—in this case, the United States.

they are for mail within the United States and its territories and possessions. (US territories and possessions include places such as Guam and Puerto Rico.)

[FACT]

Postal Fun Facts

- Benjamin Franklin became the United States' first postmaster in 1775.
- The first postage stamps were put out in 1847. A five-cent stamp pictured Ben Franklin. A ten-cent stamp pictured George Washington.
- The Pony Express began in 1860. Scheduled airmail service began in 1918.
- The US Postal Service is the only delivery service that will go to any address in the nation. It moves mail using planes, trains, trucks, cars, boats, ferries, helicopters, subways, floatplanes, hovercraft, T-3s, streetcars, mules, snowmobiles, bicycles, and feet.
- A sorting machine reads the delivery barcode and sorts letters at a rate of 36,000 pieces per hour.
- The US Postal Service Web site (www.usps.com) is an online post office. It's open for business 24 hours a day, seven days a week. And it's the most-visited Web site in the federal government.

Security Issues

Today, security is a huge concern for the US Postal Service. That includes providing for the safety of the mail, postal customers and workers, and people traveling on airplanes that carry mail. There are two key rules for security:

1. **Weight:** Mail weighing more than 13 ounces must be taken to a post office and given to a worker at the service counter. If it's dropped into a mailbox, it will be returned to the sender.

2. **Hazardous materials:** A lot of mail is moved by airplane. Materials shift and shake during travel, and there are also changes in pressure and temperature. These conditions can make many common household and consumer products dangerous. Because of this, the following materials cannot be sent through the mail: alcohol, perfume, nail polish, flea collars, spray cans, bleach, paint, matches, batteries, fuel, dry ice, mercury thermometers, cleaning supplies, glue, and fireworks.

Regular Services

Service	Things to Mail	General Time and Cost
First Class	Letters, postcards, and printed materials other than books and *periodicals*	Usual method of mailing—most items arrive within a few days
Standard Mail	Items weighing less than 16 ounces and bulk mailings of at least 200 pieces	Less costly than First Class but slower delivery
Parcel Post	Packages, including large boxes	Packages are priced according to weight—delivery is slower
Express Mail	Mostly documents	Rush service—can be delivered the next day
Priority Mail	Printed materials and packages up to 70 pounds	Fast delivery but not as fast as Express Mail

Periodical

A kind of publication that comes out on a regular basis, such as daily, weekly, or monthly. Newspapers and magazines are examples of periodicals.

Special Services

Service	Description	More Information
Special Handling	Careful handling of First Class and Priority Mail letters and packages	For breakable, fragile items
Registered Mail	Provides the sender with a mailing receipt; delivery is tracked	The item's value is declared—postage is priced according to value
Certified Mail	Provides the sender with a mailing receipt and *confirmation* of delivery	For items such as notices that require a response or involve an action
Delivery Confirmation	Provides the sender with the date and time the item was delivered	For items such as notices
Media Mail	For books, printed music, CDs, DVDs, and other recordings	Packages are priced according to weight
Insured Mail	Provides protection for valuable packages	The cost of insurance is based on the item's declared value

Confirmation

Proof that something happened as expected.

CHAPTER **4**

Parks and Recreation

Picture a public park on a golden August afternoon.

Two teenagers whack a tennis ball back and forth across a net. A group of friends chat while their puppies *romp* in an area called the "dog park."

The smell of freshly mowed grass accompanies the buzz of a Parks Department lawnmower. A family spreads an early supper on a picnic table.

Three toddlers wade in a bubbling fountain. Joggers pass by on the

Recreation
An activity done for fun and enjoyment.

Romp
To run and play in a carefree manner.

Well-groomed
Well taken care of. Kept in good shape.

well-groomed trail that winds around the duck pond.

Cheers and shouts carry from the softball field, where a city-league team is winning the championship. A happy couple exchange wedding vows in the rose garden.

Public parks serve many citizens in many ways.

Benefits of Parks

- **Health:** Parks provide space and programs for play and exercise. People of all ages go to parks to improve their health and fitness.

- **Community:** Parks add to the beauty of neighborhoods. They also offer places to meet friends, family, and neighbors. Many parks have athletic and social activities for youth, adults, and seniors. Providing activities for youth even helps reduce crime.

- **Environment:** Providing so-called green spaces helps clean the air. These spaces also soak up rain and melted snow, and they provide wild, open places for animals.

- **Economic:** Parks create jobs and increase the value of nearby property. Parks also attract visitors from out of town.

Department of Parks and Recreation

Most towns and cities have a Department of Parks and Recreation. It uses money from taxes to develop and maintain public parks and to support their activities and programs.

Check out the listings from the city of Lynnwood's Parks and Recreation Department.

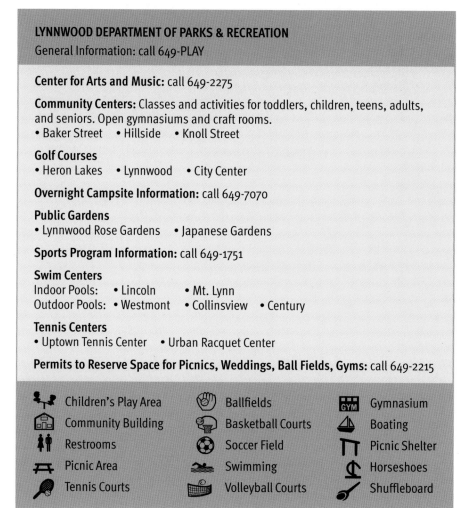

LYNNWOOD DEPARTMENT OF PARKS & RECREATION
General Information: call 649-PLAY

Center for Arts and Music: call 649-2275

Community Centers: Classes and activities for toddlers, children, teens, adults, and seniors. Open gymnasiums and craft rooms.
• Baker Street • Hillside • Knoll Street

Golf Courses
• Heron Lakes • Lynnwood • City Center

Overnight Campsite Information: call 649-7070

Public Gardens
• Lynnwood Rose Gardens • Japanese Gardens

Sports Program Information: call 649-1751

Swim Centers
Indoor Pools: • Lincoln • Mt. Lynn
Outdoor Pools: • Westmont • Collinsview • Century

Tennis Centers
• Uptown Tennis Center • Urban Racquet Center

Permits to Reserve Space for Picnics, Weddings, Ball Fields, Gyms: call 649-2215

Children's Play Area		Ballfields		Gymnasium	
Community Building		Basketball Courts		Boating	
Restrooms		Soccer Field		Picnic Shelter	
Picnic Area		Swimming		Horseshoes	
Tennis Courts		Volleyball Courts		Shuffleboard	

Taking a Stroll in Boston

One of the most well known city parks in the United States is in Boston. It's called the *Esplanade*, which is a French word meaning "a place where people walk along a shore." Boston's Esplanade lies along the Charles River and is about six miles long. The park was created in several stages by filling in marshy land. That work began in the late 1800s.

Today, an estimated 2 to 3 million people visit the Esplanade every year. Some of them come to hear the Boston Pops Orchestra. It performs every summer at Hatch Shell, which is a performance stage. Other visitors enjoy the park's many features, including the following:

6 miles of walkways and
    bike paths
5 miles of riverbank
3 boat landings
6 docks
3 boathouses
2 playgrounds
1 wading pool
3 softball fields

1 T-ball field
5 youth soccer fields
1 tennis court
2 food-and-drink stands
10 memorials and statues
9 footbridges for getting into
    and out of the park
266 park benches
1,900-plus trees

From Humble Beginnings

Women's tennis champions Venus and Serena Williams learned to play on public courts. They grew up in a suburb of Los Angeles, California. Gangs ran the area. The tennis courts were in bad shape. The cement was crumbling, and the nets were sometimes missing.

But the Williams sisters learned to play there. Their father started teaching them to play when they were three and four. He had learned about tennis from reading books and watching videos.

Today, Venus and Serena help children who remind them of themselves. The sisters help raise money and teach classes at the Southeast Tennis and Learning Center in Washington, DC. One of the rules is that students must do their homework to take tennis lessons.

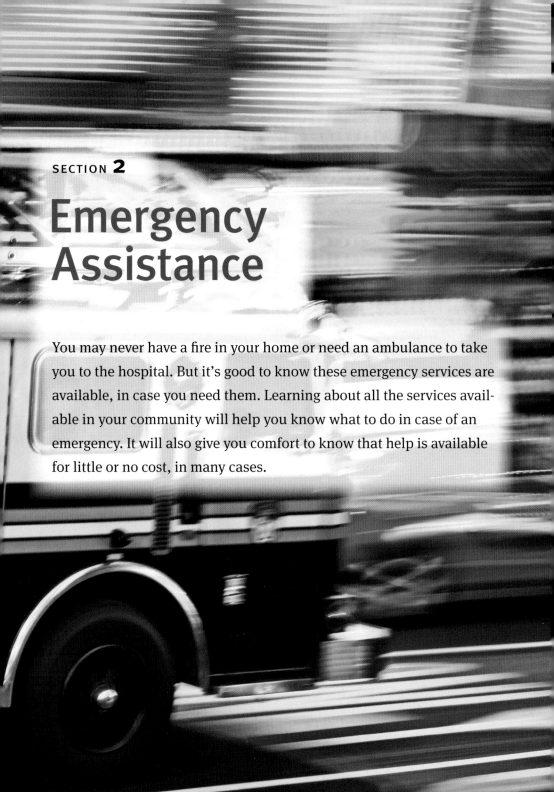

Emergency Assistance

You may never have a fire in your home or need an ambulance to take you to the hospital. But it's good to know these emergency services are available, in case you need them. Learning about all the services available in your community will help you know what to do in case of an emergency. It will also give you comfort to know that help is available for little or no cost, in many cases.

Getting Help on a Terrible Night

Donnie woke up at 3 a.m. to shouts of "Fire! Fire!" He could also hear people running down the hall of the apartment building. Some were shouting at others to hurry. Others were calling out for friends and family members. Everyone seemed in a panic!

Donnie woke up his roommates, and they hurried out of the apartment. They could smell smoke when they stepped into the hall. From what they could tell, the fire was two levels above on the top floor of the building. But it was spreading fast, they heard someone say.

Just as the roommates got outside, three fire trucks pulled up. The firefighters jumped off the trucks and immediately got to work. Within minutes, they'd hooked up the hoses and were spraying water on the blazing building.

Several ambulances and police cars pulled up, too. The police officers moved the building's residents out of the way of the firefighters. The medical workers provided oxygen to a few people who had breathed in smoke. Thankfully, no on was hurt.

After the fire was put out, the resident were told they couldn't go back into the building. In fact, they would have to stay out for at least

a couple of days. But they were told they had a place to stay, if they needed one. A community organization provided housing for people in need. Another organization provided clothing, food, and other necessities.

Donnie and his roommates were amazed to know all this! They'd never thought about what they would do if they found themselves without a home. But they were happy to know others had thought about it and were ready to help.

CHAPTER **1**

Emergency Medical Services

What should you do when you need emergency help fast? The best
thing to do is to contact your local emergency medical services (EMS).
In most communities, this
means dialing 9-1-1 on your
telephone.

Emergency medical techni-
cians (EMTs) *respond* rapidly

Respond
To provide what's been
asked for.

to these calls. They give first aid at the scene. They also provide quick transportation to a hospital. Depending on the community, methods of transportation might include ambulances, helicopters, boats, or airplanes.

The type of EMS available to you will depend on where you live. In many rural communities, volunteer teams work with the local fire department. In many cities, EMS is part of the police or fire department. In other cities, separate EMS departments are operated by the local government or run by private agencies.

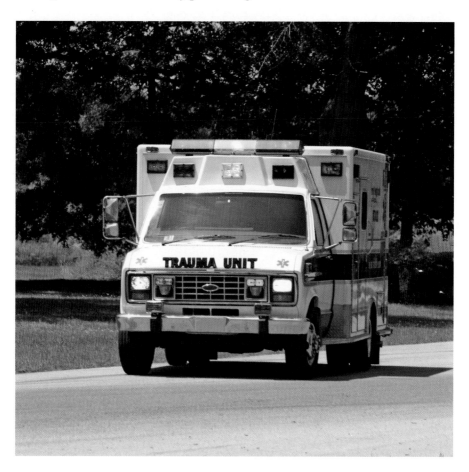

How to Call 9-1-1

Read the following transcript of a 9-1-1 call. Take note of the important details the caller provides:

CALLER: This is Maggie Russell. I'm calling from 555-3330. I just found my sister on the floor, and I can't wake her up. We live at 4621 West 47th Street in apartment 21. We're on the first floor of the Pearl Court building. It's one block west of Center Mall on the corner of Center Avenue and 47th.

9-1-1 DISPATCHER:
Maggie, I've got help on the way. They'll be there in a few minutes. Tell me, how old are you? And how old is your sister?

> **Dispatcher**
> Someone who answers telephone calls asking for help and sends the needed assistance.

CALLER: I'm 15 years old. My sister Mia is 16.

9-1-1 DISPATCHER: Is your sister breathing? Does she have a pulse?

CALLER: She's breathing, but not very much. I can feel a pulse in her wrist and neck. But she's not moving, and she's very pale.

9-1-1 DISPATCHER: Maggie, you're doing great! I want you to cover your sister with a blanket. And I have a few more questions. *Don't hang up!* Stay on the line with me until the help gets there. OK?

Checklist for 9-1-1 Callers

The checklist below lists details callers should give when dialing 9-1-1.

Review Maggie's call. Check off all the information she provided. How did she do?

9-1-1 Call Checklist

☐ Caller's name

☐ Caller's phone number

☐ Exact location help is needed, including street number, apartment number, floor

☐ Directions, **landmarks**, and cross streets

☐ Description of the emergency, including signs and **symptoms**

☐ Number of people needing help

Landmarks

Well-known or commonly seen sites. Examples of landmarks are statues, bridges, and well-known buildings.

Symptoms

Signs of illness.

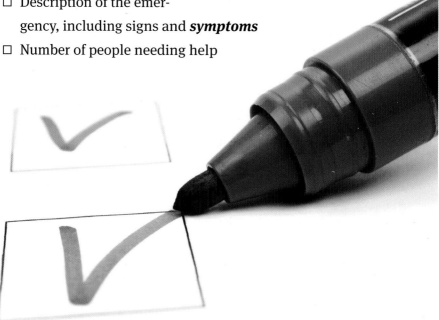

[FACT]

A Brief History of 9-1-1

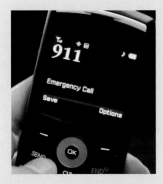

In 1967, the US government decided to set up a single, nationwide number to make emergency calls to police departments. The Federal Communications Commission (FCC) worked with the nation's largest telephone company to set up that number. The first 9-1-1 call in the United States was made in 1968. Gradually, communities across the nation set up 9-1-1 service. And over the years, technology updates have improved the speed and handling of 9-1-1 calls.

When Not to Call 9-1-1

- For help in a situation that isn't an emergency
- For information from the police
- To find the phone number of another city department
- When you're bored and want to talk
- To pay a traffic ticket
- To get emergency service for a pet
- To play a joke

Calling 9-1-1 as a joke is against the law in most states. But if you call 9-1-1 by mistake, don't hang up. Explain what happened so the dispatcher will know there's no emergency.

CHAPTER 2

Police and Fire Department Services

What Does the Police Department Do?

The following paragraph is the ***mission statement*** of one city's police department:

Police Department Mission Statement
To maintain safety and security by working in partnership with the community; to enforce laws, prevent crime, and ***safeguard*** the rights of all people; to promote trust in the police.

According to the US Bureau of Labor Statistics, there are about 884,000 police officers and detectives in the United States:

→ 79% are employed by local governments

→ 11% work for state police agencies

→ Various federal agencies employ police and detectives

What do all these police officers do?

→ Patrol officers cover *beats*, which are specific areas like neighborhoods. These officers work their beats on foot, in squad cars, or on motorcycles. In some places, they patrol on bikes or on horseback.

→ Traffic officers keep the roads safe by directing motorists and **pedestrians**. They enforce traffic laws and are on the scene at accidents.

Mission statement	**Safeguard**	**Pedestrian**
A description of a group's goals or purposes.	To defend or protect.	Someone who is traveling on foot.

→ Detectives are the police department's investigators. They work with scientists in crime labs to examine fingerprints, weapons, and other evidence.

→ Officers in the juvenile department handle cases involving people under 18. These officers work with youth to protect their rights and prevent juvenile crime.

Police departments in large cities have special units:

→ Search-and-rescue teams find people lost in wilderness areas or at sea.

→ ***Negotiators*** come on the scene when criminals hold people against their will. The negotiators try to reach a peaceful settlement to a difficult situation.

→ Bomb squads search for and disarm explosives. Specially trained dogs sometimes work with bomb squads.

Negotiator

Someone who works with people in a conflict to reach an agreement.

→ SWAT (Special Weapons and Tactics) teams are trained to respond in dangerous situations.

→ Computer crimes units investigate illegal activities done using computers.

Police departments also work closely with members of the community. For example, they support neighborhood watch programs, which teach people how to protect their own streets and homes from crime.

Start a Neighborhood Watch

1. Gather and organize as many neighbors as possible. Include everyone you can: young and old, single and married, renters and homeowners.

2. Contact your local police department. Invite an officer to a meeting to discuss crime prevention.

3. Discuss neighborhood concerns. Then make an action plan for handling the problems.

4. Agree on a way for neighbors to communicate. Make a map with people's names, addresses, and phone numbers.

5. Hold regular meetings to keep everyone informed and involved.

6. Follow through with your action plan.

Computer Forensics

The word *forensics* refers to the technology used to provide evidence in a court of law. *Computer forensics* involves looking for evidence on a computer. A lot of that evidence is material that's been created or saved on the computer, such as financial records, photographs, and e-mails. This kind of material can usually be found even if it's been hidden on or deleted from the computer. Finding other kinds of evidence involves tracking what the computer's user has been doing—for instance, browsing the Internet, sending and receiving e-mails, and copying or deleting files. Specialized software and training are needed to find much of this evidence.

What Does the Fire Department Do?

Here's the mission statement of a local fire department:

Fire Department Mission Statement
To improve life in our community by providing high-quality fire and rescue service, an excellent fire prevention program, and a firefighting force able to respond to all emergencies.

Firefighters do more than protect people and property from fire:

→ Firefighters also respond to nonfire emergencies. For example, they free people trapped in fallen-down buildings and car accidents. They rescue victims of earthquakes, floods, and storms.

→ Many fire departments provide emergency medical services (EMS). When people need help, the fire department sends quick, highly skilled medical assistance.

→ Fire departments investigate the causes of fires. They try to figure out if illegal activities are involved, such as arson (setting a fire on purpose).

→ Firefighters also inspect buildings to make sure they meet fire codes. *Fire codes* are laws for how buildings must be constructed to make them safe in case of a fire.

→ To prevent fires before they start, firefighters teach fire safety to school and community groups.

CHAPTER **3**

Help in a Crisis: Hotlines and Shelters

At some time in your life, you'll probably face a problem you don't know how to handle. Maybe you'll have a problem with drugs or alcohol. Or maybe you'll simply need help with your homework.

Hotlines

Whether you're facing serious troubles or everyday worries, you can get help by calling or e-mailing **hotlines**. You can also find information on Web sites.

> **Hotline**
>
> A service that can be contacted to get information or help in an emergency.

Different hotlines provide a wide range of services. The people who work at hotlines are well trained and highly experienced. Look at the following list to see what kinds of help are provided:

AIDS Information, Center for Disease Control and Prevention

Answers questions about AIDS/HIV prevention, testing, and health care

   Toll-free phone number: 1-800-232-4636

   Web site: www.cdc.gov

   Web site: www.aidsinfo.nih.gov

American Council on Alcoholism Helpline

*Offers educational materials and gives **referrals** for alcohol treatment programs*

   Toll-free phone number:

      1-800-527-5344

   Web site: www.aca-usa.org

Referral

A recommendation or suggestion of whom to call for service or help.

Provides information and referrals for health problems and emergency issues

Toll-free phone number: 1-800-RED-CROSS

Web site: www.redcross.org

American Red Cross

In 1881, an American woman named Clara Barton started an organization called the American Red Cross. Her goal was to help people who were in need and had nowhere else to turn. Earlier in her own life, Barton had risked her safety to help soldiers on the Civil War battlefields. She went on to lead the Red Cross for 23 years, until she was 82 years old.

The American Red Cross helps out in crises that affect communities. It's run by volunteers. The group's mission statement has two goals: to help victims of disasters, and to train people to prevent, prepare for, and respond to emergencies.

Offers counseling and referrals in drug and alcohol abuse emergencies

Toll-free phone number: 1-800-662-HELP

Web site: www.samhsa.gov

Child Find Hotline

Helps in locating lost children and provides help directly to lost children

Toll-free phone number: 1-800-I-AM-LOST

Web site: www.childfindofamerica.org

Dial-a-Teacher

A free, after-school service that answers questions in many languages

Long-distance phone number: 1-212-777-3380

Web site: www.uft.org

Dial-a-Teacher

Some states, local communities, and teachers' groups offer Dial-a-Teacher services. A call to one of these services will provide a teacher to help with homework. Most of the services offer help Monday through Thursday afternoons, and some also offer help in the evenings. Many offer help both by phone and online, and instruction is often available in several languages.

To get help with your homework, go online and search for "Dial-a-Teacher." Then type in your state or city to see if this service is available in your area.

National Association for Children of Alcoholics

Offers information and support to children of alcoholics

    Toll-free phone number: 1-888-554-COAS

    Web site: www.nacoa.net

National Child Abuse Hotline

Gives help to victims of child abuse and provides information and referrals

    Toll-free phone number: 1-800-4-A-CHILD

    Web site: www.childhelp.org

National Hotline for Missing Children

Helps locate missing children

    Toll-free phone number: 1-800-843-5678

    Web site: www.missingkids.com

Notice from the list that most hotlines have toll-free phone numbers. These numbers let you call long-distance for free. Also check your phone directory or the Internet for the local phone numbers of these hotlines.

Finally, keep in mind that most hotlines provide service 24 hours a day, seven days a week. In most cases, help is available any time you might need it.

Shelters

At times, talking to someone at a hotline isn't enough. Physical help is needed. In most communities, human services organizations provide **shelters**. These organizations are listed online and in the phone book.

Some shelters protect people from violent friends and family members. Others provide food and beds for people who are homeless. Still others offer somewhere to stay while going through a difficult time.

Many of the organizations that run shelters are government **sponsored**. Others are services run by religious groups. The people who work at shelters may be paid employees or volunteers.

Shelter

A place that provides safe, temporary housing for people in need. Many of the people who stay in shelters are homeless or in some kind of danger.

Sponsor

To be responsible for or provide guidance to.

CHAPTER 4

Legal Aid and Public Defenders

Legal Aid

An elderly couple, Mr. and Mrs. Stedman, found themselves with a legal problem. Their apartment had leaking pipes and a dangerous heating system. The landlord refused to make repairs. Because the Stedmans couldn't afford a lawyer, they called the legal aid agency.

Legal aid is a program that offers free legal services for people who can't pay lawyers' fees. Legal aid agencies are often supported by federal, state, and local governments. They may also be sponsored by law schools, lawyers' associations, and money donated by individuals.

Legal aid agencies usually **counsel** people with low incomes, along with senior citizens and people with disabilities. Legal aid lawyers offer help with common legal matters, such as divorce, bankruptcy, job or consumer problems, health care **disputes**, and **discrimination**. These lawyers generally don't handle criminal cases.

Counsel

To give advice to, especially legal advice. Lawyers are sometimes called *counselors*.

Dispute

A disagreement or conflict.

Discrimination

Unfair treatment based on a personal quality, such as race or ethnicity, gender, age, or income level.

Many legal aid agencies have hotlines that provide legal counseling and referrals over the phone or by e-mail. They may hold *clinics* that offer information about common problems, such as landlord/tenant disputes and child custody disagreements.

Clinic

A meeting set up in a law office or agency that anyone can come to and get legal help for little or no cost. Often, the help is provided by advanced law students being supervised by an attorney.

Public Defenders

Legal help for people who can't afford lawyers is also available from public defenders. A public defender is a lawyer that's paid by the state to defend people who are accused of crimes but can't afford legal help. The government provides this help because everyone who's arrested has the right to have an attorney.

When criminal suspects are arrested, they are advised of their rights. The arresting police officer uses language like this: "You have the right to consult with a lawyer . . . If you cannot afford a lawyer, one will be appointed for you, if you wish."

Most public defenders handle only criminal cases. They have two goals: (1) to preserve and protect the rights of all people and (2) to make sure the court offers justice to all.

Public defenders don't work for or with the police. (*District attorneys* work with law enforcement.) Instead, a public defenders' role is to safeguard the rights of people accused of crimes.

How to Get a Public Defender

1. Contact the local public defender's office. Find out what the requirements are.

2. Ask the judge to appoint a lawyer to represent you.

3. Prove that you have a low income. Bring in paycheck stubs or tax returns. If someone else helps pay your expenses, he or she may need to state that in a letter.

4. Give the public defender's office the papers you received in court. This will help the office assign the best lawyer for your case. It will also help the lawyer get started quickly.

5. Provide contact information, so your lawyer can reach you easily. If this information changes, let your lawyer know.

[FACT]

The Miranda Warning

Do you know your rights in case you're ever arrested? Those rights were provided by a famous court case in 1966. It involved a man named Ernesto Miranda, whom the police forced to confess to a crime. After hearing this case, the US Supreme Court ruled that police must tell someone the following things when arresting him or her:

- "You have the right to remain silent."
- "Anything you say can and will be used against you in a court of law."
- "You have the right to speak with an attorney and to have an attorney present during any questioning."
- "If you can't afford an attorney, one will be provided for you at the government's expense."

Police must tell people these rights by saying what's known as the *Miranda warning*.

Services for Workers

Most people expect to work their whole lives. They plan for the future and look forward to retiring in their old age. But sometimes, life doesn't follow the plan! People lose their jobs or get hurt at work. And when they lose their income, they often face other problems, too. The government provides services to support people in tough times. Learn

Getting Help When It Hurts

It all happened so quickly! One minute, Luca was carrying a tray full of dirty dashes through the restaurant. And the next minute, he was lying on the floor, feeling dazed.

"Wow, what happened?" Luca asked. "I guess I slipped on something."

"Yeah, the floor's really wet there," his co-worker said. "Somebody spilled a tray of drinks and didn't wipe it up very well. Sorry you fell. But you're OK, right?"

Actually, Luca wasn't OK. His left shoulder and arm really hurt. He'd slammed them hard against the floor. He finished working his shift that night, but he was in pain.

The next morning, Luca went to the doctor. He found out he'd hurt his shoulder pretty badly. Nothing was broken, but he'd have to keep his arm in a sling for several weeks.

"Great! Now I can't work," Luca grumbled to himself. "What am I going to do for money?" Not only did Luca have his regular bills to pay. But getting hurt meant he'd have medical bills to pay, too.

Luca stopped by the restaurant to tell his manager, Glenn, that he wouldn't be able to work for a while. After Luca explained how he got hurt, Glenn said the restaurant was responsible for helping him. Businesses have a kind of insurance that pays employees who get hurt at work.

Glenn was also concerned about why Luca slipped and fell. The restaurant could get in trouble if there were more accidents. Plus, no one should have to worry about getting hurt on the job, Glenn said.

CHAPTER **1**

Getting a Social Security Number

*"The Social Security program . . . represents our commitment as a society to the belief that workers should not live in dread that disability, death, or old age could leave them or their families **destitute**."*
—FORMER US PRESIDENT, JIMMY CARTER

History of Social Security

The very first Social Security number was issued to John Sweeney, Jr. But it wasn't the lowest number. That went to Grace Owen. How did that happen? Do some research and find out!

What happens when US workers retire or are unable to work for some reason? How do they and their families meet their financial needs?

In 1935, the US Congress passed the Social Security Act. Since then, Social Security payments have helped replace people's income that's been lost due to retirement, unemployment, disability, or death.

Americans become *eligible* to get Social Security payments by working for a certain period. Employers and workers fund the program through payroll taxes.

Destitute

Not having any of the basic necessities in life, such as food, clothing, and shelter.

Eligible

Being able to or having the right to.

How Does Social Security Work?

- Workers pay taxes for Social Security. The rate is 7.65% of a person's earnings.

- Employers match this amount, and all the money goes into a fund.

- As you work and pay taxes, you earn Social Security credits —up to 4 a year.

- You need at least 40 credits (10 years of work) to get paid Social Security after you retire.

- You get paid after you reach retirement age—age 67, if you were born after 1959.

- The more you pay over your working life, the more you receive after you retire.

- On average, Social Security pays about 40% of what someone earned while working.

Being Part of Social Security

Almost all US workers must become part of the Social Security system. You'll need to get a Social Security number before you start earning income. Your personal number will be printed on a Social Security card. That number will be used to track your earnings and contributions and to figure your payments.

After you get a Social Security number, be very careful with it. Keep your Social Security card in a safe place with your other important papers.

Social Security and Identity Theft

Criminals can use your Social Security number to get other personal information about you. Then, they can apply for credit cards in your name and not pay the bills. You can end up with a lot of problems, including a bad credit history.

To avoid this bad situation, follow these tips:

- Guard your Social Security number carefully.

- Don't carry your Social Security card with you. And don't write it on a piece of paper and keep it in your wallet.

- If someone asks for your Social Security number, ask why he or she needs it. Also ask what will happen if you refuse to give it. Then decide if it's safe.

Getting a Social Security Number and Card

How do you get Form SS-5, the application for a Social Security card? Contact your local Social Security office. (Call 1-800-772-1213 for information.) You'll also find the SS-5 form, as well as other Social Security information, on the agency's Web site (www.ssa.gov).

Can Social Security Keep Paying Americans?

The Social Security taxes being paid by workers today are being spent to pay people who are already retired. When the program started in the 1930s, there were many more workers than retired people. Also, people didn't live as long as they do now. That means that today, many retired people receive much more money than is paid into the system. And the number of retirees will soon be greater than the number of workers. By 2018, Social Security will be paying out more than it receives each year.

How can Social Security be "fixed"?

- Raise other taxes
- Borrow money from the public
- Reduce government spending on other programs
- Reduce Social Security payments

When you apply for a Social Security number, you'll need the following information:

→ Your mother's Social Security number (if she has one and you know it)

→ Your father's Social Security number (if he has one and you know it)

→ Original or **certified** documents that prove your age, identity, and US citizenship or lawful alien status. These can include any of the following:

   —Hospital record of your birth

   —Adoption record

   —Driver's license

   —School ID card

   —Passport

   —Military record

   —Certificate of Citizenship or Naturalization

Certified
Authorized as being accurate or legal.

Take or mail the SS-5 form and the required documents to a Social Security office. You can find the location of the nearest office in the phone book or on the Web site. After the office receives your application, it will take about two weeks for you to receive your card.

CHAPTER **2**

State Employment Office

Benjamin had been working for a concrete waterproofing company. But after months of dry weather, business fell off. The owner had to let go some employees, including Ben.

Now, Ben needs money to live on until he finds a new job. So, he's turning to his state employment office for help.

Every state in the United States has an employment office that's *financed* by federal taxes. Ben finds his state's office online and contacts the nearest location.

What Is Unemployment Insurance?

Ben files a ***claim*** to receive unemployment insurance *benefits*, or payments. Unemployment insurance protects workers who don't have jobs but are ***actively*** seeking employment. It pays benefits for a limited amount of time.

Each week, when Ben files a claim, he'll need to show that he's trying to find work. The employment office will also help him in his job search.

Finance	**Claim**	**Actively**
To provide the money for.	A request for payment.	In an eager or busy way.

[FACT]

How Does Unemployment Insurance Work?

- Unemployment benefits vary state by state.

- On average, unemployment pays about half the amount you earned in your former job.

- While you're out of a job and actively seeking work, you'll receive a check each week. You'll get checks for between 26 and 30 weeks—about six or seven months.

- If you're still jobless at the end of this period, you may qualify for the extended benefits program. It will provide payments for another 13 to 20 weeks.

- During very bad economic times, the government may pay unemployment benefits even longer.

Each state *regulates* its own employment office, so specific rules and programs may vary. Most offices have what's called a *job order desk*. Employers call in with job openings they want to have listed. Unemployed workers, like Ben, contact the office for information about available jobs.

Regulate

To control or supervise according to rules or laws.

How Can You Find the Right Job?

Ben tells the state employment office all about his work experience, education, interests, and skills. This will help office staff match him with job openings on their list. They can also give Ben tips on applying for jobs and going to interviews.

In addition, most state employment offices offer information about job training and schools. On the employment office Web site, Ben has found a lot of information, including local, statewide, and national job listings.

The state employment office helped Ben when he was laid off. And getting unemployment benefits allowed him to have some income between jobs.

With the help of the job placement staff, Ben was soon back at work at a new job—and earning a paycheck, once again.

Tips for Unemployed People

1. Update or create your résumé, which outlines your education and work experience.

2. Look online and in the newspaper every day to review classified ads of available jobs.

3. Apply for jobs and go to as many interviews as you can.

4. Look for ways to cut expenses and save money.

5. Find a part-time job to earn money.

6. Avoid watching TV or sitting at the computer all day.

7. Find things to do that don't cost money, both at home and away.

8. Stay in touch with family and friends. Let them help!

9. Don't feel hopeless or angry about your situation.

10. Spend some time thinking about what you have and what you want in life.

CHAPTER 3

Federal Safeguards

Department of Labor (DOL)

The Department of Labor (DOL) is a part of the federal government. It protects the *welfare* of the United States' many millions of workers.

Welfare
Health and happiness.

The Employment Standards Administration (ESA) is the largest agency within the DOL. The ESA defends workers' rights. It enforces laws for minimum wage, overtime work, and child labor. The ESA also oversees family and medical leave—programs that let people take time off with pay. And the ESA promotes equal job opportunities.

Child Labor Laws

Throughout much of US history, children worked long hours. That work often put them in dangerous places, such as factories and mines.

Then, in 1938, Congress passed the Fair Labor Standards Act. It outlawed most hiring of children under age 16. Youth ages 16 and 17 could take jobs that involved no safety hazards. Children ages 14 and 15 could work part-time outside school hours, if the job was safe.

[FACT]

Minimum Wage Increases Over the Years

The Fair Labor Standards Act also requires employers to pay workers a minimum wage. Over time, Congress has increased that wage to keep up with *inflation*, which is an increase in the average level of prices.

The following chart shows what the minimum wage was in different years. It also shows what that wage would have been worth in 2010:

Year	Minimum Wage (per hour)	Value in 2010 Dollars
1940	$0.30	$4.67
1945	$0.40	$4.85
1950	$0.75	$6.79
1955	$0.75	$6.10
1960	$1.00	$7.37
1965	$1.25	$8.65
1970	$1.60	$8.99
1975	$2.10	$8.51
1980	$3.10	$8.20
1985	$3.35	$6.79
1990	$3.80	$6.34
1995	$4.25	$6.08
2000	$5.15	$6.52
2005	$5.15	$5.75
2010	$7.25	$7.25

Occupational Safety and Health Administration (OSHA)

OSHA (pronounced OH-shuh) is another agency in the DOL. It's responsible for overseeing safe and healthy working conditions.

To better understand how OSHA operates, imagine that you're taking a factory tour with OSHA inspector Walter McGuire.

Inspector McGuire is making a routine visit to the Better Box Company. He does a walkthrough of the offices and factory, checking off safety requirements:

☐ Does the company meet requirements for fire prevention, *hazardous* waste disposal, and worker *exposure* to chemicals?

☐ Does the building provide proper stairway railings and lighting?

☐ Are factory workers given protective clothing, such as hard hats and safety eyeglasses? And are they expected to wear it?

Hazardous
Risky or dangerous.

Exposure
An unprotected or uncovered contact with something dangerous.

After making a visual check of the factory, Inspector McGuire asks to see written safety manuals and guidelines. He encourages the company to set up a safety committee with members from all departments.

The Better Box Company is a responsible employer, so Inspector McGuire finds only a few minor violations. "You need bigger signs over the fire exits," the inspector recommends. "And the door on this electrical panel is loose and should be replaced."

Inspector McGuire writes a report of his findings. He allows the Better Box Company a period of time to correct its violations. But if they don't make the improvements, they can be fined.

Like most employers, the Better Box Company wants to provide a healthy, safe, accident-free workplace. Concerned business owners value OSHA visits and recommendations. They are anxious to meet the safety requirements set down by the federal government.

[FACT]

Work-Related Injuries, Illnesses, and Deaths (2009)

Nonfatal Work-Related Injuries and Illnesses
   Total cases: 3,277,700
   Cases involving days away from work: 965,000
   Cases involving sprains, strains, and tears: 379,340
   Cases involving back injuries: 195,150
   Cases involving falls: 212,760

Fatal Work-Related Injuries
   Total cases: 4,551
   Cases involving highway accidents: 866
   Cases involving falls: 605
   Cases involving homicides (murders): 462

CHAPTER 4

Filing for Workers' Compensation

Accidents can happen anywhere. Jesse broke his ankle while working at the Better Box Company. During the four weeks he was off the job, he collected workers' *compensation* benefits.

Compensation

A payment to make up for something, such as loss, suffering, or injury.

What Is Workers' Compensation?

Workers' compensation is an insurance program that's usually overseen by the state. (In some cases, it's overseen by the federal government.) Workers' comp, as it's sometimes called, covers medical costs for workers who are hurt on the job or become sick because of working **conditions**.

Workers' comp also provides pay to cover lost wages. And in cases of job-related deaths, workers' families receive benefits.

In most states, employers are required to provide workers' compensation insurance. Usually, employers pay the costs through taxes or insurance payments.

Conditions

The qualities or status of a place. In the workplace, conditions include qualities that make people comfortable and safe. Examples include proper lighting, clean and dry floors, and properly working equipment.

[FACT]

Who Pays for Workers' Compensation?

Employers pay the money that funds workers' compensation insurance. How much a specific employer pays depends on several things:

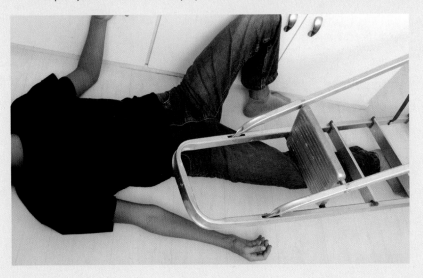

- **Type of business:** Businesses that do high-risk work pay more than businesses that do low-risk work. For instance, a construction company pays more than an accounting firm.

- **Size:** Large companies with high earnings and many employees may pay a lower rate than small companies.

- **Injury history:** The more injuries that have occurred at a company, the more it will pay.

Workers' Compensation FAQs

Jesse wasn't sure how to file a workers' compensation claim. He also had some other questions about how workers' comp operates. Here are the answers to these and other frequently asked questions (FAQs):

Q: What medical benefits are covered?

A: Workers' compensation covers medical services and supplies for job-related injuries. That includes doctor and hospital bills, physical therapy, medicine, and mental health counseling.

Q: What is a *temporary disability*?

A: Jesse was able to return to work after his ankle healed. So the payments he received while he was off the job were called *temporary total disability compensation*.

Q: What if I can't return to my old job because of my injury?

A: Workers' compensation programs may help retrain injured workers. The goal is to find them safe jobs that fit their physical abilities, education, and employment backgrounds. Some people who can't return to work because of a work-related injury or illness receive *permanent total disability compensation*.

Cheating the System

Some workers try to make false workers' compensation claims. They cheat the system to get more money and more paid time off. These cheaters cost employers a lot of money.

How do workers cheat the workers' comp system?

- By saying they were injured at work when they were really injured somewhere else.

- By saying that an injury is more serious than it really is.

- By making up an injury that's hard to prove as false.

- By claiming their job caused an injury that actually happened long ago.

- By stretching out their recovery time away from work longer than necessary.

Q: What information will I need when I file my claim?

A: To file a workers' comp claim, you must notify your employer of your on-the-job injury or illness. Then, you have to complete an application form.

Be ready to give the following information:

→ Name

→ Gender

→ Date of birth

→ Social Security number

→ Mailing address

→ Home and/or work phone numbers

→ Occupation or job title

→ Date of accident or first symptoms of illness

→ Description of accident

→ Type of injury/illness and part of body affected

Q: What if my claim is denied?

A: If your claim is ***denied***, you have the right to protest. For most jobs, you can ***contest*** the decision at your state's workers' compensation office. If you work for the federal government or have a job such as coal miner or longshoreman, check with the US Department of Labor. (See http://www.dol.gov/owcp for more information.)

Denied

Turned down or refused.

Contest

To challenge or oppose, as used here.

Services for Citizens

Some US citizens take for granted the opportunities they have. For instance, they don't vote to elect leaders and pass laws. Other people are eager to become US citizens! They leave their homelands and come to the United States in search of better lives. Find out what it takes for these people to live and work in the United States. And find out how to fulfill the dream many of them share: to become a US citizen.

The Newest American

Mula's big day was finally here: She was going to become a US citizen! She'd take part in a ceremony at the courthouse later this morning. Along with many others, she would pledge her loyalty to her new country.

Mula had dreamed of becoming a citizen for a long time—six years, in fact. She'd come to the United States with her family when she was just 15. They had fled their homeland because of continual war there. Mula's parents had wanted her and her brothers to grow up somewhere safe.

The last six years hadn't been easy. Mula had struggled in school for a while. At first, she didn't speak English very well, so school had been difficult. She'd also had a hard time making friends. She was pretty shy. But soon, she fit right in with the other students. She even went out for a couple of sports—something a girl never could have done in her homeland.

Since graduating from high school, Mula had worked with her parents in their small grocery store. She was trying hard to save enough money to go to college. She dreamed of becoming a teacher. She wanted to do a job that helped other people.

Mula knew that as a US citizen, she had both rights and responsibilities. She'd learned that in a class about US history and government. After she took the class, she took a test. Passing the test is one of the requirements for becoming a citizen. So is being able to read, write, and speak English.

Mula was proud of becoming an American. She knew she'd remember this day forever.

CHAPTER 1

Vital Records

The government keeps records of basic events in the lives of all its citizens. It uses these **_vital_** records to analyze and understand the population. The data show changes and trends that help the government plan for the future.

You need vital records, too. For instance, you need a birth certificate to get a passport. You need to **_verify_** your age when applying for a driver's license or a job. And filing a life insurance claim may require a death certificate.

Vital
Related to or necessary for life.

Verify
To prove as true or accurate.

Ordering Vital Records

In most states, county offices keep vital records. You can often order records by going online or by calling the county's Department of Vital Records.

The three kinds of vital records most people want copies of are birth certificates, death certificates, and marriage certificates. The lists that follow tell what a county or state might require when you order these documents. Check with your local vital records office to find out its specific requirements.

Birth Certificates

When requesting a birth certificate, include the following information:

Date of request

Full name

Date of birth

Place of birth

Mother's maiden (unmarried) name

Father's name

Your relationship to the person (if the certificate isn't your own)

Reason the record is needed

Your name and address

Your driver's license number and state

Your signature

Death Certificates

When requesting a death certificate, include the following details:

Date of request

Full name of the deceased

Date of death

Place of death

Your relationship to the person

Reason record is needed

Your name and address

Your driver's license number and state

Your signature

Getting a Safe Deposit Box

The best place to store vital records is in a safe deposit box at a bank. How can you get one?

1. Talk to your bank about renting a box. Many banks give discounts to existing customers.

2. Decide what size box you need. If you plan on storing only documents, then a small box will be fine.

3. Fill out and sign a box rental agreement. Anyone else you want to be able to open the box should sign it, too.

4. Pick a safe place to store the key to the box. Make sure it's a place you'll remember and be able to get to easily.

What to Keep in a Safe Deposit Box

Passports
Birth certificates
Death certificates
Marriage certificates or licenses
Divorce agreements
Custody agreements
Adoption papers
Citizenship records

Military service papers
Other court-recorded documents
Wills
Financial and insurance
   documents
Deeds and titles to property
Contracts and other agreements

Marriage Certificates

When requesting a marriage certificate, include the following information:

Full name of husband

Full maiden (unmarried) name
   of wife

Date of marriage

Place of marriage

Your relationship to person
   (if this isn't your marriage
   certificate)

Reason record is needed

Your name and address

Your driver's license number
   and state

Your signature

Fees and Restrictions

The fees required to order vital records vary by county and state. In California, most fees are less than $20 for a record search and a certified copy of a document.

Also keep in mind that many records are restricted. That means they're available only to the individual and his or her

immediate family or legal representative. States' restrictions on birth and death certificates last for 100 and 50 years, respectively.

[FACT]

Tracing Your Family History

Many people use vital records to trace their family history. These records are usually on file with county governments. So, your search for information will be easier if you know the state and county where a relative was born, married, or buried.

If you don't know the state and county, contact the Social Security Death Index (SSDI). It's a huge database that includes almost everyone who's died in the United States since 1962. The SSDI provides individuals' Social Security numbers and birth and death dates. And it sometimes provides addresses.

Also contact the Centers for Disease Control and Prevention (CDCP). This federal organization provides information about whom to contact for records in each state. Go online to www.cdc.gov/ncs/w2w.htm.

Resources for Genealogists

A *genealogist* is someone who traces family history. Many organizations provide services and information that can aid genealogists in their work. Newspapers may have birth, marriage, and death announcements and other articles of interest. If you have immigrant ancestors, look to the countries they came from for even more information.

- Newspaper records: www.NewspaperArchive.com
- National Archives: www.archives.gov/research/genealogy/index.html
- Genealogy Web sites: www.Ancestry.com, www.FreeGenealogyTools.com, www.VitalRecordsUS.com, www.WorldVitalRecords.com

CHAPTER **2**

The Right to Vote

In 1971, the federal government lowered the voting age to 18. It had been 21 for many years. Americans pushed to lower the age so that young adults could vote.

At the time, the United States was fighting the Vietnam War. Eighteen-year-olds could be drafted to serve in the military, but they couldn't vote! This didn't seem right to many Americans, so the law was changed.

Having the Right to Vote

The right to vote is guaranteed by the Twenty-Sixth *Amendment* to the US *Constitution*:

> *"The right of citizens of the United States, who are eighteen years of age or older, to vote shall not be denied . . . by the United States or by any State."*

If you are an 18-year-old US citizen, you are eligible to vote in federal, state, and local elections. To *exercise* this right, you must register with your local election bureau. And whenever you change your name, address, or political party, you'll need to reregister, or update your information.

Amendment	Constitution	Exercise
A change or addition to a legal document.	The set of beliefs and values on which a government is based.	To act on or fulfill a right or responsibility.

[FACT]

Who Votes the Most in the United States?

- **Age:** Seniors 65 and older
- **Education:** College graduates
- **Income:** People with household incomes of $50,000 a year or more
- **Region:** Residents of the Midwest
- **Permanent address:** People who have lived in the same place for at least five years
- **Property status:** Homeowners
- **Marital status:** Married people
- **Employment status:** Job holders

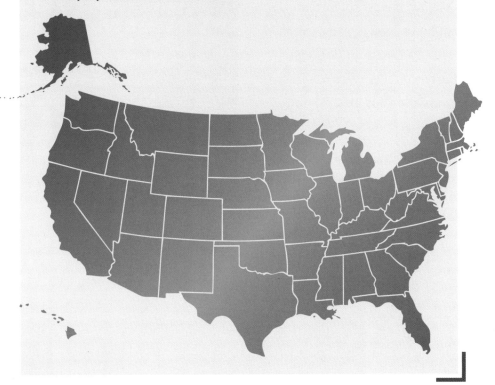

[FACT]

Changing Times

Americans don't exercise their right to vote as much as they did a half-century ago. In 1964, 96% of voting-age citizens who were registered voters actually voted in elections. But in 2008, only 70% of eligible, registered voters cast their ballots.

Today, many more people of color can vote than in times past. In 1965, the Voting Rights Act outlawed discrimination, which had blocked many African Americans from voting. In 2004, most registered voters from the four largest US population groups said that they voted:

Population Group	Registered Voters Who Voted
Whites (non-Hispanic)	89%
African Americans	87%
Asian Americans	85%
Hispanic Americans	82%

Registering to Vote

Registering to vote requires filling out a form similar to one below from the state of Oregon.

Voter Registration Application

Before completing this form, review the General, Application, and State specific instructions.

Are you a citizen of the United States of America? ☐ Yes ☐ No	This space for office use only.
Will you be 18 years old on or before election day? ☐ Yes ☐ No	

If you checked "No" in response to either of these questions, do not complete form.
(Please see state-specific instructions for rules regarding eligibility to register prior to age 18.)

1 — (Circle one) Mr. Mrs. Miss Ms. | Last Name | First Name | Middle Name(s) | (Circle one) Jr Sr II III IV

2 — Home Address | Apt. or Lot # | City/Town | State | Zip Code

3 — Address Where You Get Your Mail If Different From Above | City/Town | State | Zip Code

4 — Date of Birth ___ / ___ / ___ Month Day Year | **5** — Telephone Number (optional) | **6** — ID Number - (See Item 6 in the instructions for your state)

7 — Choice of Party (see item 7 in the instructions for your State) | **8** — Race or Ethnic Group (see item 8 in the instructions for your State)

9 — I have reviewed my state's instructions and I swear/affirm that:
- I am a United States citizen
- I meet the eligibility requirements of my state and subscribe to any oath required.
- The information I have provided is true to the best of my knowledge under penalty of perjury. If I have provided false information, I may be fined, imprisoned, or (if not a U.S. citizen) deported from or refused entry to the United States.

Please sign full name (or put mark) ▲

Date: ___ / ___ / ___ Month Day Year

If you are registering to vote for the first time: please refer to the application instructions for information on submitting copies of valid identification documents with this form.

Please fill out the sections below if they apply to you.

If this application is for a **change of name,** what was your name before you changed it?

A — Mr. Mrs. Miss Ms. | Last Name | First Name | Middle Name(s) | (Circle one) Jr Sr II III IV

If you were **registered before but this is the first time you are registering from the address in Box 2,** what was your address where you were registered before?

B — Street (or route and box number) | Apt. or Lot # | City/Town/County | State | Zip Code

If you live in a rural area but do not have a street number, or if you have no address, please show on the map where you live.

C
- Write in the names of the crossroads (or streets) nearest to where you live.
- Draw an **X** to show where you live.
- Use a dot to show any schools, churches, stores, or other landmarks near where you live, and write the name of the landmark.

NORTH ↑

Example | Route #2 | ● Grocery Store | Woodchuck Road | Public School ● | X

If the applicant is unable to sign, who helped the applicant fill out this application? Give name, address and phone number (phone number optional).

D

Mail this application to the address provided for your State.

The elections office will mail you a card to let you know your registration was received. In some states and counties, you must go to the **polls** to cast your vote. Your registration card will list a precinct number, which says what part of the voting district you live in. Having that number will help you locate your polling place.

In many states, more and more elections offer vote-by-mail ballots. They're sometimes called *absentee ballots*. Registered voters receive ballots and cast votes through the US mail.

Polls

Places where people vote and votes are counted.

CHAPTER **3**

Legal Immigration:
The USCIS and Green Cards

The United States is a nation of immigrants. In fact, American culture is sometimes described as a "melting pot" or a "patchwork quilt" because of its ***diversity***. Today, government agencies and programs help US immigrants live, work, and receive rights and benefits.

Words to Know

Reading and learning about immigration will make much more sense to you if you understand the meanings of these words:

→ **Immigration:** The act of coming to a new country to live

→ **Immigrant:** Someone who moves to a new country

→ **Native:** Someone who was born in the country

> **Diversity**
>
> Variety or difference.

US Immigration Timeline

Year(s)	Country	Number of Immigrants to US
Before 1790	British Isles	475,000
	Africa	300,000
	Germany	100,000
1790–1820	British Isles	120,000
	Africa	85,000
	France	40,000
1820–1880	British Isles	4.8 million
	Germany	3 million
	Eastern Europe	1 million
1880–1930	Italy	4.6 million
	Eastern Europe	4 million
	British Isles	4 million
1930–1965	Germany	940,000
	Canada	900,000
	Mexico	610,000
1965–2000	Mexico	4.3 million
	West Indies	1.5 million
	Philippines	1.4 million

→ **Citizen:** Someone who is a legal resident of the country.

→ **Alien:** Someone who isn't a citizen; someone from a foreign country.

→ **Naturalization:** The act of becoming a citizen.

→ **Refugee:** Someone who has been forced to leave his or her country (for instance, because of war).

→ **Deported:** Forced to leave a country by an official order.

→ **Asylum:** Protection provided to a refugee.

→ **Green Card:** A document that grants an alien the legal right to live and work in the United States permanently.

→ **Visa:** Official written permission to be in a country.

US Citizenship and Immigration Services (USCIS)

The US Citizenship and Immigration Services (USCIS) is a federal agency. It's part of the Department of Homeland Security (DHS).

The mission of the USCIS is to provide help to aliens who want to legally live and work in the United States—either temporarily or permanently. Specifically, the USCIS does the following:

→ Oversees those who apply to become naturalized citizens.

→ Helps US citizens and permanent residents who want to bring close relatives to the country.

→ Supervises the process that allows individuals from other countries to work in the United States.

→ Helps US citizens who want to adopt children from other countries.

→ Offers and maintains **humanitarian** programs.

→ Provides educational services about American culture to immigrants.

Other federal agencies handle immigration enforcement and border security. For more about the USCIS, go to www.uscis.gov/portal/site/uscis.

Humanitarian

Concerned with human welfare.

[FACT]

Illegal Immigrants

Not all immigrants are in the country legally. In 2010, the Department of Homeland Security (DHS) estimated that 10.8 million illegal immigrants were living in the United States. The DHS also provided these details about the group:

- 4.2 million (39%) had entered the United States in the year 2000 or later.
- 8.6 million (80%) were from the North American region, including Canada, Mexico, the Caribbean, and Central America.
- 6.6 million (62%) were from Mexico.
- 2.6 million (24%) settled in California, and 1.8 million (17%) settled in Texas.
- 6.8 million (63%) were between the ages of 25 and 44.
- 6.2 million (57%) were males, and 4.6 million (43%) were females.
- The 2010 population of illegal immigrants had dropped from the peak of 11.8 million in 2007.

Green Cards

A "diversity visa" is a Green Card program that aims to make sure a variety of countries are represented in each year's immigration. These Green Cards go only to aliens from countries with a history of low immigration to the United States.

There is a yearly **lottery** for these visas, which is run by the US Department of State (DOS). Fifty thousand people are selected each year. To be eligible, the individual must meet two requirements:

Lottery

A drawing in which each item or person has an equal chance of being selected.

1. Have a high school education or equivalent

2. Be a native of a qualifying country

In some cases, employers can help alien employees get Green Cards. And families of Green Card holders can also receive visas. They can live permanently in the United States or choose to apply for citizenship.

Refugees who are granted asylum and immigrants who marry US citizens can get visas, too.

[FACT]

Who Can Immigrate?

Reason for Immigration	Relationship to Sponsor	Number of Immigrants Allowed per Year
Family of US citizen	Husbands and wives, unmarried children under 21, parents	No limit
Family of US citizen or lawful permanent resident	Children (all ages, married or not), brothers and sisters	260,000–480,000
Employment in the United States	—	140,000 (including dependent family members)
Refugee	—	80,000

Green Card Information Web Sites

www.usa-green-card.com

www.us-immigration.com

www.travel.state.gov/visa

CHAPTER 4

Becoming a Citizen

Twenty-three-year-old Rosa moved to the United States when she was 17. When she first arrived, she took English classes and completed high school. Her favorite subject was US history. Then, she attended two years of community college. Now, she works in the accounting department of the Better Box Company.

Ways of Becoming a US Citizen

There are two ways a person can become a US citizen: by birth or by naturalization. People who are born in the United States *automatically* become citizens. People who move to the United States must become naturalized citizens.

> **Automatically**
>
> Acting or happening without planning or thinking about it.

Naturalized citizens have all the rights and duties of someone born in this country, with one exception: They can't serve as president or vice president of the United States.

Rosa is eager to be naturalized as a US citizen. She downloaded an application form from the US Citizenship and Immigration Services (USCIS) Web site. She found information about the naturalization process and citizenship requirements, too.

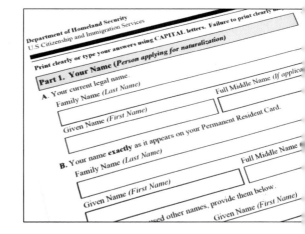

Who Seeks US Citizenship and Why?

In 2010, nearly 620,000 immigrants became naturalized US citizens. The largest number of them lived in California, followed by New York and Florida. And they came from the following countries, in order by number of naturalizations:

- Mexico (67,062)
- Philippines (35,465)
- China (33,969)
- Vietnam (19,313)

What reasons do people give for wanting to become naturalized citizens?

- To have the right to vote
- To be able to bring other family members to the United States
- To protect their children's right to stay in the United States

Requirements for Becoming a US Citizen

Some important facts that Rosa learned are listed below. From what you know about Rosa, do you think she qualifies to become a US citizen?

Applicants for naturalization must meet these requirements:

→ **Age:** The individual must be at least 18 years old. In many cases, children under age 18 automatically become US citizens if one or both of their parents become naturalized.

→ **Character:** While living in the United States, the applicant has to have shown good moral ***character*** and followed the ideas of the US Constitution.

- → **Residency:** The applicant has to have lived in the United States for at least five years. For *spouses* of US citizens, the period is usually three years.

- → **Language skills:** The individual must be able to read, write, and speak English.

- → **Knowledge of country:** The individual must show knowledge and understanding of US history and government.

- → **Ceremony:** The applicant must take part in a swearing-in ceremony and swear an oath of *allegiance*. In taking this final step toward citizenship, applicants promise to give up loyalty to any foreign government, to support and defend the US Constitution and laws against all enemies, and to serve in the armed forces if asked to.

Spouse
A partner in marriage. A husband or wife.

Allegiance
Loyalty or commitment.

Character
The qualities that make up and guide an individual, especially qualities such as values and morals.

US Citizenship Test

The process of becoming a citizen includes passing a citizenship test. It shows that someone has a basic knowledge of the United States. The test has two parts, each with three sections:

1. **Civics:** US government, the rights and duties of citizens (from the US Constitution), and US history

2. **English language:** Reading, writing, and speaking

Taking and passing the test is one of the final steps before being sworn in as a naturalized citizen. The entire application process can take anywhere from six months to four years or more. The time needed depends on how busy the USCIS office is and on whether a person's application has any problems.

The United States Naturalization Oath

"I hereby declare, on oath, that I absolutely and entirely renounce and abjure all allegiance and fidelity to any foreign prince, potentate, state, or sovereignty of whom or which I have heretofore been a subject or citizen; that I will support and defend the Constitution and laws of the United States of America against all enemies, foreign and domestic; that I will bear true faith and allegiance to the same; that I will bear arms on behalf of the United States when required by the law; that I will perform noncombatant service in the armed forces of the United States when required by the law; that I will perform work of national importance under civilian direction when required by the law; and that I take this obligation freely without any mental reservation or purpose of evasion; so help me God."

Word List

abuse
access
accident
accurate
accuse
administer
agency
alien
allegiance
alternate
amazed
ambulance
amendment
analyze
ancestor
anxious
application
assault
assign
assistance
athletic
attorney
attract
authorize
automatically
available

ballot
benefits

candidate
catalog
ceremony
certificate
certified
challenge
champion

checklist
chemical
civics
co-worker
commitment
compensation
conditions
confirmation
conflict
constitution
consult
consumer
contact
contest
contribution
conversation
cooperation
counsel
courage
coverage
criminal
crisis
culture
customer

dangerous
data
dazed
dedicated
defendant
defender
degree
delete
delivery
deny
describe
design

destination
details
detective
develop
difficult
directory
disability
disaster
discount
discrimination
discuss
dispatcher
dispose
dispute
distress
diversity
document
domestic
donate
duty

eager
earnings
economic
elect
eligible
emergency
employ
enforce
entertainment
environment
equivalent
especially
estimate
evidence
examine
exception

exchange
exhibit
expensive
experienced
explosive
exposure
extended

fatal
federal
fee
festival
finance
foreign
former
fragile
fund
future

graduate
groomed
guaranteed
guidance
guidelines

hazardous
homeland
hotline
household
housing
humanitarian
humble

identity
immigrant
impress
income

Word List

inflation
information
informed
inspect
institution
instruction
insurance
interview
involve
issue

jobless
juvenile

keyword

lawyer
librarian
license
limited
lottery
loyalty

maintain
manager
materials
medical
minimum
minority

naturalization
necessities
negotiator

oath
occupation
organization

overtime

package
participate
partnership
passport
pedestrian
performance
permanent
pharmacy
physical
pledge
policy
political
poll
premiums
preserve
prevent
principle
process
product
program
protect
protest
publication

qualify
qualities

rapidly
receipt
recommend
recovery
recreation
reference
referral
region

register
regulate
relationship
relative
religious
replace
represent
request
rescue
research
resident
resources
respond
responsibilities
restrict
retire
retrain
risky
role
routine
rural

safety
scheduled
security
select
session
settlement
severe
shallow
shelter
shift
signature
similar
sites
situation
specialized

specific
sponsor
staff
statement
status
substance
supervise
support
swear
symptom

technique
technology
temporary
tenant
transcript
transportation
treatment

unemployment
update

valuable
variety
verify
victim
violation
violent
visa
visual
vital
volunteer

weapon
welfare
workplace

Index

Index

Index